Meditation
The 13 pathways to happiness

First published by O Books, 2006
O Books is an imprint of John Hunt Publishing Ltd.,
The Bothy, Deershot Lodge, Park Lane, Ropley, Hants,
SO24 0BE, UK
office1@o-books.net
www.o-books.net

Distribution in:

UK and Europe
Orca Book Services
orders@orcabookservices.co.uk
Tel: 01202 665432
Fax: 01202 666219 Int. code (44)

New Zealand
Peaceful Living
books@peaceful-living.co.nz
Tel: 64 7 57 18105
Fax: 64 7 57 18513

USA and Canada
NBN
custserv@nbnbooks.com
Tel: 1 800 462 6420
Fax: 1 800 338 4550

Singapore
STP
davidbuckland@tlp.com.sg
Tel: 65 6276
Fax: 65 6276 7119

Australia
Brumby Books
sales@brumbybooks.com
Tel: 61 3 9761 5535
Fax: 61 3 9761 7095

South Africa
Alternative Books
altbook@peterhyde.co.za
Tel: 021 447 5300
Fax: 021 447 1430

Text copyright Jim Ryan 2006

Design: Jim Weaver

ISBN-13: 978 1 905047 72 7
ISBN-10: 1 905047 72 X

A CIP catalogue record for this book is available from the British
Library.

Printed in the UK by Ashford Colour Press

Meditation

The 13 pathways to happiness

Jim Ryan

BOOKS

Winchester, U.K.
New York, U.S.A.

Contents

All your thoughts break their bonds
your mind transcends limitations,
your consciousness expands
in every direction,
and you find yourself in a new,
great and wonderful world.
Dormant forces, faculties and talents
become alive, and you discover yourself
to be a greater person be far
than you ever dreamed
yourself to be.

PATANJALI

Introduction

Each of us stands alone, facing our own life's journey.

Most of us with a questioning mind and an empty heart.

We seem to be continually journeying for the answers to one and attempting to fill the other.

We do it physically through exploring the world around us, mentally through theory or science, or imaginatively through the creations of culture. But none of these journeys truly satisfy. We're still searching, trying to find our own Holy Grail. Often, we can't even describe what we're looking for.

Spirituality teaches us that the answers we need can be found within. We can reconnect with our long lost truths, our deeper awareness and true experience by turning our thoughts inwards.

The method we use is meditation.

Maybe, this for you conjures up something magical and mystical. Well it can be that. But it can also increase your awareness, develop your understanding and improve your health and well being.

Through its practice, we can access our active energies of peace and love and wisdom, so empowering and transforming our self confidence, thinking and interactions.

This book has been written as a clear and simple guide for those who wish to learn and practice meditation; and for those long time practioners, showing another facet of the jewel that is spiritual consciousness.

It provides a step by step guide on how to access and develop your vast inner potential. Also on how to share the benefits that come to us and to our relationships.

It has been written on the basis of my long time interest and experience in metaphysics over a period of 25 years.

The book is dedicated to my teacher Dadi Janki and my good friend Shiv Baba.

Big thanks to Sue Emery and Divina Lloyd for advice and guidance.

1 Path of search

There are two main parts of an orange; the outer skin and the inner fruit. The former is dry, tasteless, often bitter and of little use. Yet the latter is juicy, sweet and full of goodness.

In the same way, life for many of us today is like living on the skin of an orange. Existence is difficult, with much labour, not much return and very little sweetness. And, tragically, most of us are totally oblivious of any solution or even the need for a solution, due, to the massive influence of the surrounding world.

Obsessed, infatuated and trapped in the external, all awareness, all memory of the spiritual, inner worlds becomes lost.Yet, as with our orange, this is also the simple message of spirituality. Go within and you'll find what you seek, what you have been longing and thirsting for – the fruit of true and pure experience.

Looking at our overburdened planet with its huge numbers and its vast complexity of parts and forms, all presenting such a profusion of choice and a myriad of moral dilemmas, it is no wonder there is so often a confusion in our purpose and a dilution of our higher ideals. As a result, we compromise these and begin to accept things for which we are unsuited. In so doing, we lose ourselves; and in becoming lost, we become afraid, confused and quickly bereft of courage and of all hope. Our life feels dry, empty; and everything we do seems devoid of meaning and direction. We become like a rudderless ship, desperately searching for love's safe haven.

It is only when we leave our surface world and go deep within, that we can resolve our dilemma. By stepping onto the inner plane, into the dimension of silence – it is then we have the possibility of reaching our goal. For in meditation, the mind can withdraw itself from life's illusions and direct its thinking inwards, to find and to re-create the experience of true love.

It's interesting to note that when we try to make some sense of our roller-coaster world, subconsciously and naturally, we often begin to think more subtly in order to try to find meaning and direction. In doing so we begin to touch our soul's inner world, thereby stirring deep, unlimited, spiritual feelings and memories that in turn, begin to trigger experiences of truth, love and natural well being.

Why don't we step aside for a few moments, go into silence and experience that calmness, that centre of peace and love?

Meditation

Let us now move away from the demands
and the needs of our chaotic world,
and slip into our inner world,
into the quiet, still room of the mind.
It is a place, a space of calm, stillness and peace.
Here, I can let go of my concerns, worries and constant fears.
In this dimension of silence,
in this plain of peace,
The incessant voices grow distant and quiet.
And in this arena of inner calm and soft serenity,
my racing thoughts begin to slow down,
begin to lose momentum
and are absorbed into that inner peace.
I am surrounded by silence,
by peace.
And that soft vibration soothes my mind and calms my thoughts.
and I am held in that spell of tranquillity,
I am bathed in the inner light of the inner self.
And I float and drift in this sea of silence,
in this sea of peace.
For here the waves of the world cannot come.
and I feel light and free and calm.

2 Path of confusion

For many, the demands of relationships and lifestyle become too great. We seem to be working overtime just trying to cope and, in consequence, many of us become casualties, through stress or nervous disorders.

In trying to alleviate and compensate for this lack of fulfilment, we constantly attempt to manufacture solutions and distractions, as we try to placate our incessant thirst for newness and experience. Or we lose ourselves in the fantasy worlds of videos, novels and lottery wins, or escape the bland and the superficial, through excessive food, drink and drugs.

For some, there is the temptation to just pack their bags and run away, but, like the boomerang, we have to return, and eventually face our fears, responsibilities and our world.

So where and what is our solution to our present-day tragedy of ancient Greek proportions?

This dichotomy of the pulls of the inner and outer worlds is nicely illustrated by the story of the fisherman and the businessman.

A very rich industrialist was horrified one day to find a fisherman lying lazily beside his boat, smoking a pipe. "Why aren't you out fishing?" asked the industrialist. "Because I have caught enough fish for the day", said the fisherman. "Why don't you catch some more?" "What would I do with them?" "You could earn more money," said the businessman. "With that you could have a motor attached to your boat and then go into deeper waters and catch more fish. Then you would make enough money to buy bigger and better nets. These would bring you more fish and more money. Soon you would be able to buy one or two more boats, even a fleet of them. Then you would be rich like me!" "What would I do then?" "Why, then you could really enjoy life." "What do you think I am doing right now?"

So we leave our contented fisherman. But to counter the contention that love and fulfilment comes from material gain, the following questions will give us a different perspective.

Why am I unfulfilled?
What am I rejecting?
What am I looking for?
What is the purpose of my life?

The very asking of these questions helps us to put the brakes on the runaway train of our life.

Once we begin to question our actions, our way of living and our essential needs, we begin to set in motion the incredible internal mechanism of the soul.

Once programmed correctly, like a computer, it will give us the answers and insight that we need in order to put our life back on track and so become more worthwhile.

> "If you are confronted with a problem and you cannot see an immediate answer, assume that your subconscious has the solution and is waiting to reveal it to you. If an answer does not come, turn the problem over to your deeper mind prior to sleep. Keep on turning your request over to your subconscious until the answer comes. The response will be a certain feeling, an inner awareness, whereby you know what to do. Guidance in all things comes as the still small voice within."
>
> BRIAN ADAMS – *HOW TO SUCCEED*

For so long, we have been wandering in life's cul de sacs unaware of why and what we are doing. Now, through spirituality, we have the opportunity to start to do the right things, as Rumi puts it:

> "The master said there is one thing in this world which must never be forgotten. If you were to forget everything else, but were not to forget this, there would be no cause to worry; while if you remembered, performed and attended to everything else, but forgot that one thing, you would in fact have done nothing whatsoever. It is as if a king had sent you to a country to carry out one specific task. You go to the country and you perform a

hundred other tasks, but if you have not performed the task you were sent for, it is as if you have performed nothing at all. So man has come into the world for a particular task, and that is his purpose. If he doesn't perform it, he will have done nothing."

RUMI – *TABLE TALK*

To accomplish and make something of our lives, we need to align and connect with our own unique purpose and direction. To help us, a simple approach can be used.

Steps to find our purpose

Go into silence.
Allow other thoughts to subside.
Ask your question: What's my purpose?
Have faith in what comes.
Think deeply on the content.
Act upon it.

"Once you begin the journey towards a life of purpose, you enter the realm of real magic."

WAYNE DYER

This simple process of standing back and observing is very effective in helping to sort out our often confused and discordant feelings and thoughts. To see what is and what is not important enables us to become more focused and clear. This creates a more positive and powerful consciousness that is our key to resolving confusion.

In times past, man explored the highways of the outer worlds, seeking his own particular idealised form of perfect love. Gradually he became trapped in its illusions and glamour, and because of that, lost awareness of the inner path to true experience.

There is a story of a man who found an eagle's egg and put it in the nest of his hens. The eaglet hatched with the brood of chicks and grew up with them.

All his life the eagle did what the chickens did, thinking he was also a chicken. He scratched the earth for worms. He clucked and cackled. And he would thrash his wings and fly a few feet into the air.

Years passed and the eagle grew very old. One day he saw a magnificent bird far above him in the cloudless sky. It glided in graceful majesty among the powerful wind currents.

The old eagle looked up in awe. "Who's that?" he asked.

"That's the eagle, the king of the birds," said his neighbour.

"He belongs to the sky.

We belong to the earth – we're chickens."

So the eagle lived and died a chicken, for that's what he thought he was.

TRADITIONAL

So has it been the same for us?

Maybe, we remember a first experience of a life that was centred in peace and natural harmony. As time passed, due to interaction and influence, we forgot our inner world and we became attracted and then attached to the outer world of form and matter. In course of time we became separated from our original nature, and thus moved away from true awareness and perception.

When things started to go wrong, having lost our spiritual identity and needing support and help, we then started to unsuccessfully search for truth and love in the words, in the company of others, and within the physical world itself. Believing what we heard and saw, unguided and unaware, we followed those steps, spoke the same words, yet, because these were not ours, we couldn't change, we couldn't fly.

However, like the eagle, the solutions, the answers, were always with us. We just weren't aware. Now with knowledge, we can understand and accept our true spiritual identity and we can consciously redirect our awareness inwards and access our own internal reservoir of pure experience.

This is Meditation.

3 Path of awareness

Incredibly, it seems that a lot of our time has been spent in a futile search. We have been misdirected and misinformed, deluded into thinking that our most precious and long sought-after treasure of love was somewhere outside ourselves when all the while, it was travelling with us, a part of us.

This confusion has led us to a whole tangled web of misunderstandings and wrong perceptions, moving us further and further away from our true metaphysical centre.

By seeing and accepting the forms of the outer world, seeing our faces in the reflecting mirror of another, we have forgotten our spiritual reality. We have become men and women, we have become our roles, we have become the builder, the baker, the candlestick maker. We become them because we see and accept and think we are them, and so then become trapped in their limitations.

This association with the form of the body has caused the externalisation of our awareness and the loss of our spiritual nature, so forcing us to live on the perimeter of our feelings, where we are left to surf in the often turbulent waves of our physical emotions. As a consequence, our experiences then become shallow and superficial, leaving us empty of that deep, inner strength which is necessary to deal with the demands of our difficult world.

However, when we start to think more profoundly about ourselves, it then becomes possible to differentiate between reality and falsehood, between the role we play and who we really are. As the driver of a car is evidently not the car, but one who controls and operates and makes it move, so the soul is the spiritual operator of the body – it sees and hears and feels through its portals and organs and senses. Just as the actor is separate from his part, we can now realise the difference between the body and the one who uses the body.

As we begin to absorb and accept the difference between the physical and the spiritual, we start to allow our inner world to slowly filter through to our everyday awareness and as a result, we gradually start to become more detached, enabling us more easily to let go of the habit of external identification, shifting us naturally onto a more subtle level of perception, so opening the door to the inner, energy centre of the self.

Let us embrace these ideas with some thoughts of reflection.

Take them into your subtle mind.

Hold and then for moment experience each idea, allow them to resonate with your inner self.

Meditation

I shift my awareness from the outer worlds
of form and movement and change.
I enter the softness of my inner world,
I open myself to what is real and true,
to what I know I need,
and I allow my love-centre heart,
to embrace me,
to soothe,
caress
and fill my emptiness,
I am calm,
I am still,
I am centred,
surrounded by the vibration of peace,
by the energy of light,
by the feelings of love.
These experiences hold me,
fill me,
I feel light,
in harmony.

4 Path of understanding

WHO AM I?

If I am not just my physical role and form, we move towards the idea that I am a subtle, spiritual being, which is expressing itself through the costume of the body, just like an actor playing and adopting a role, but, who is of course, not the part or person he's playing.

And what then is the nature and form of the soul?

We can agree that the self is certainly a subtle energy, and that it manifests through thought, awareness and action. Isn't it true that when we move away from love and light and peace, we immediately feel at odds with ourself, uncomfortable and naked, wanting alignment again?

It's because we are these qualities, they are part and parcel of who we are, so then, we are what we long for – that is, love, light, peace and wisdom.

With this understanding and acceptance we now can begin to unfold our inner world experience. But we need first to stabilise the thoughts that will be necessary for our journey into these inner realms.

Try this very easy exercise. It will enable you to control the volume and speed of your thoughts and so help to centre your awareness. As a result you'll become more calm, easy and alert.

Use these suggested thoughts. You may even like to record them and play them back to yourself.

Reflection

I think of myself as light,
I am a living spiritual energy,
a shining light point,
a star point of pure consciousness.
I am not my body,
or my role.
I am a living, spiritual energy,
a shining light point,
a star point of pure consciousness.

Slowly repeat these thoughts. Break the sentence down. Then think deeply about each aspect and try to experience it by holding it in your awareness. We can take this experience further by focusing now on our main foundation energy of love.

You may wish to first visualize your soul form energy as a soft, beautiful and radiant light, or just work purely with thoughts – either is fine.

Reflection

I am pure energy,
I am a living being of love,
my form and nature is of love,
I experience that love,
I become that love,
I am that love.
This pure,
soothing
powerful,
loveful energy,
flows around and through me,
there is nothing but love.
This is my true nature.

As you go into this experience, try to stay with it, and even if your thoughts slip away, return to it, keep your mind centred in that lovefulness. Hold it, observe it, experience it, be it. Allow that love to develop, flourish and influence.

In the same way, let us take another of our innate qualities and explore and integrate its effect into our conscious energy field. Again repeat these phrases slowly in your mind, and try to experience each thought by holding it in your awareness.

Reflection

I am a serene,
peaceful soul,
my nature is also of peace;
I emerge from that peace,
I experience that peace,
that peace flows in and around me,
becomes part of me,
is me,
I am that peace.

Let us link all these thoughts and use them as a vehicle to take us deeper into the experience of our true self;

Meditation

I withdraw my thoughts and awareness from the interaction of
    the day,
I journey into the inner world of my own being,
Into the inner sanctuary of inner healing,
here in my own inner space,
I am safe and secure,
Nothing can touch or harm me,
I am centred in silence,

Free,
And in this light, detached state of ease and serenity,
I am aware of my true form and identity,
I am the living, pure and eternal energy,
The shining soul of radiant light,
And now I emerge and experience my original nature,
My original qualities; those of love and light and peace,
The purest fountain of love emerges, flows through me, fills and
    surrounds me,
I become that love,
I am that love,
And the light of peace emerges
I go into that peace,
I become that peace
I am that peace
I am that light, that love, that peace, that bliss,
that natural state of wisdom and true being.
And I am focussed, centred and empowered
in this aura of pure consciousness,
aware that that my form is of light,
my nature is of peace,
my being is of love.

5 Path of realization

What is soul consciousness?

So often in today's world, our mind becomes trapped by desires, multiple worries and countless fears, causing our thoughts to spin in a whirlwind of speculative, possible scenarios. Our thoughts in this mayhem rub together like dry bamboo, creating a thought fire, in which it becomes difficult to think, understand or make sense of what's going on around us. As a result, we misinterpret, make mistakes and our life becomes a mess.

Yet, on our inner journey, our thoughts, attracted and held by our emergent spiritual energy, become more centred, less frenetic and eventually stilled. A calmness and peacefulness sweeps through our whole being; our breathing becomes slower, heart and pulse rate more even, and our whole body, now freed from the incessant agitation of waste thought, has space and time to regenerate. Healing and integration can now take place.

Our meditation practice is related to changing more positively the focus and content of our thinking, so creating a subtler, more refined and perceptive state of awareness. As a result we are then able to come closer and be more connected to the heart centre of our spiritual self.

Using spiritual consciousness

Present needs and demanding lifestyles have necessitated that we are able to operate on several separate mental levels at the same time – we can eat, read, keep the children seated and at the same time, talk on the phone!

We can use this same multi-functional agility to good effect in our meditation practice. With a focussed spiritual awareness, wherever we are, either working in an office or factory, preparing food, going for a walk or even having a conversation; by bringing a heightened awareness and a still, peaceful and loveful mind into every encounter, not only do we gain we clarity and perception, but we bring compassion, good feelings and love into all that we do.

So before we connect with the world, if we first set our mind in a state of loveful, soul conscious awareness, we then become fully prepared for any coming interaction. And as a result, others will certainly feel that empathy and truth and so be more likely to respond with positivity and like feeling.

Let's practice this mindset.

Meditation

I am a pure, peaceful soul.
A spiritual energy,
a being of light,
an actor,
playing a part with the costume of my body,
but I am separate from my part.
I am also the observer;
from my inner space,
I see out into the world,
I see the great play of life,
I see the other actors,
my brothers
and I realise that each one
is the shaper and creator of their part.
I cannot play their part
or change the scene.
But in my state of self awareness,
I can give support and strength.
I can send them light and love and peace.

Just before you join the company of others, keep the essence of this meditation in your awareness and then monitor the effect, observe how you and others are now relating.

To establish and make this a more natural part of our outlook, we can take this understanding into a fuller meditation practice, so that it can be absorbed deeply into our spiritual nature.

So let us set our intention and desire and step into the dimension of silence:

Meditation

I focus my awareness on my spiritual form of living energy,
the pure consciousness of the eternal soul.
I understand and experience my form as the form of light.
I am centred.
Now using my body as a costume,
a vehicle of expression,
I see through my eyes,
I hear through my ears,
I feel through my heart,
yet, I am separate from all these.
I open and extend my awareness
and connect with others around me.
They are the same as myself,
my brother souls,
who are also interacting and interrelating through their costumes
   of the body,
playing their part.
Yet, my vision is not limited to the form and the role of these
   actors;
I can now go beyond and pierce the illusion of matter and form.
I can see their true nature.
I see their virtues and qualities.
I accept and appreciate how they are,

what they are,
as they are.
Around me, too,
I see many situations,
many forms of action and reaction,
yet, I remain detached and light
peaceful and full of love.
I am not affected by any of the negative emotions I encounter.
I am the observer,
watching the scenes with love and compassion.
And now with the power of discrimination
I can choose to act when and how I wish,
with the appropriate and correct attitude.
I am peaceful,
I am light,
I am the being of love.

Through such introversion and reflection we now begin to use greater understanding, intuition and spiritual qualities to deal with the circumstances of our life.

Understanding the spiritual self

The following story shows an interesting perspective on how things can be viewed.

Two followers of an old master were arguing about the true path to God. One said that the path was built on effort and energy, and that it was necessary to give yourself totally and fully to God, following the laws precisely. The second follower disagreed , saying, that it wasn't based on effort, that's ego, but on giving oneself fully to God, opening up to inspiration and grace.

As they couldn't agree, they decided to go to their master. He listened to the first follower who praised the path of effort and who asked, is this the true path? The old master paused thought for a moment and replied, "You're absolutely right!" On hearing this the second follower was very upset, saying, surely , the true path was based on surrender, inspiration and love? The old master, paused, thought for a moment and replied, "You're absolutely right also!" Now a third follower who was there said, "But master, they both can't be right!" And the master smiled and said, "And you're right too!"

CHASSID

A lovely story that teaches us that each one of us sees reality from a very individual perspective, based upon our own body of personal wisdom and unique experiences. And that all we can do and should do for others, is to offer support when needed; and keep in our hearts good wishes and pure feelings for the success of their spiritual journey, allowing us then to concentrate on what we have to do for our own life needs.

Of course, there are times when we walk right into the middle of an argument or dispute, and with so much emotional baggage flying around, it's easy to get sucked in and become submerged and entangled in all the emotion. Yet, with our mind pre-programmed with spiritual awareness, we need no longer live on the edge of this precipice. Filled with coolness, detachment and clarity, we can become aware of things before they hit us and drag us into their turmoil. From this powerful vantage point of the spiritual observer, it becomes so much easier to be objective and unaffected by whatever is going on.

Our soul-conscious state enables us to relate in a completely un-limited way to each one's universal truth, and so we can connect with a greater degree of positive attention, co-operation and support.

Let's now prepare and empower our awareness, ready for when we connect with others:

Meditation

I withdraw into my inner space,
to my focal point,
to the seat of my true being.
Aware of my spiritual reality of the pure soul,
I feel light and free and serene.

As I have many issues and problems to understand and resolve,
I know that it is only me who can only truly appreciate
my own feelings about where I want to go and what I need to do.
In the same way,
I now have a greater understanding of those around me,
my fellow actors,
that they too are on the same journey of self discovery,
that they too are having to deal with complications and situations
just as I have to,
maybe, they're having to deal with the very same issues as I am
    facing at this moment,
so with this understanding,
with patience, tolerance and compassion,
I see and appreciate their qualities and specialities.
I see them as my brothers, friends and fellow travellers.
walking the same path,
trying in their own way,
trying their best to achieve their goals,
their dreams.
I let go of all judgement and criticism.
I give them respect and space,
space to be themselves,
to express themselves.
I have no desire to play their part
or to interfere with their role.
I stand back,
listen and reflect on what they have to say,
what they desire to achieve.
From my state of love,
I give them
my co-operation,
my support
and my blessing.

By using such thoughts, we start to build a very positive and loveful attitude, and as a consequence, we also begin to see others in that same light.

6 Path of love

Difficulties in expressing love

To understand the reasons for our difficulties in being open, aware and loveful, it's necessary to understand how our consciousness is constructed and how the parts are interrelated and affect each other. We can separate our mind state into three areas;

► Conscious Mind
► Subconscious Mind
► Unconscious Mind

The conscious mind

The conscious mind is concerned with meeting all the requirements that we need in order to exist. It's the part of our awareness that connects with the outer world and which channels information in and out. It responds by producing thoughts. The content and speed of thought of the conscious mind is directly related to our attitude and our nature, which in turn, are formulated through the influence of others, from situations and the subconscious. We hear some worrying news or experience a difficult situation, these can trigger memories and feelings in our subconscious, which might then go into overdrive, speculating and imagining, resulting in thoughts becoming fast and frenetic, creating feelings of fear and anxiety. Yet when we link with our spiritual energies, through knowledge or a subtle experience, conversely our thoughts slow down, become calmer and more lucid.

The subconscious mind

The subconscious is rather like a great recording machine, continually on, never switching off. The effects of everything that we experience and think about are etched onto its memory banks; nothing is ever lost or not recorded. So what happens is that experiences, habits and memories begin to accumulate, and as a particular activity is repeated, it starts to become a major part of our personality. In the course of our activities, as well as dealing with our own emotional upheavals, we often have to contend with many difficult and sometimes unpleasant situations. One aspect of our coping mechanism is that we then repress these feelings and thoughts into the deeper recesses of our subconscious hoping they'll go away or just disappear. But they don't, and it's when we are stressed, tired or pushed to our limits that they again rear their often unpleasant heads, bursting through from the subconscious, into our conscious mind, causing us to be irritable, fractious or depressed, giving rise, maybe, to emotional outpourings, arguments and conflicts.

This tension between our conscious and subconscious creates an overload demand on our inner resources, as we try to reconcile a multitude of emotions, leading to a great deal of stress and mental anxiety, and of course, the subsequent physical repercussions in our body.

The unconscious mind

It is here in the unconscious mind, unconscious, because we have been so long unaware of its existence, that meditation can step in and begin to really help sort out many of our complications. By focusing our awareness on this deeper part of our mind, soul being, we start to release and experience our innate energies of peace, love, bliss and light. These emerge like a fountain of pure energy, flooding the subconscious, bringing healing, resolution and empowerment to our often fractured and splintered personality, to eventually surface in our conscious mind, creating an arena of peace and lovefulness. Thus, the unconscious becomes conscious.

And that long dormant energy, that much sought after power, now, like some newly discovered treasure, begins to fill our mind and thoughts and feelings. And we start to feel light and easy, strong, aware, balanced, peaceful and loving.

Let us now experience this integration of our original and pure nature into our present consciousness.

Meditation

Letting go of the outer world,
my mind is focused and centred
on my inner reality and true centre of power.
My thoughts are completely connected,
fixed on my spiritual being;
and through a fusion of thoughts, awareness and energy,
I experience its power rising and flowing.
The incredible and pure power
of peace and love and light and bliss becomes activated,
filling every pore of my being.
Its energy and vibration resonates, heals, refreshes,
finishes the effects and echoes of past effects and old memory.
A great feeling of purity,
cleansing and newness fills me.
I feel fresh and strong and clear.

In this state of heightened spiritual experience, the soul is resonating to the beauty of its own being and something wonderful is also happening. For the first time, there is a bridge between the external world and the soul's inner spiritual state. This link is the emergent energy of the soul's original nature, as it releases a power and a vibrancy that begins to work a magic, whereby everything now becomes possible, like in this story from the Chassid, of the decaying monastery...

The old monastery had fallen upon hard times. Once a great order, with wealth and lands, now things were bad and there was only the old abbot and four elderly monks remaining; clearly it was a dying order. In the surrounding woods there was the retreat of a local rabbi, from the nearby town. The abbot, thinking that there wasn't much time left for his order, thought he would visit his old friend the rabbi, and ask him if by some chance he could offer any advice that might save the monastery.

The rabbi welcomed the abbot, but on hearing of his plight, could only commiserate with the abbot, agreeing that certainly, the spirit had gone out of the people. It was the same for him, very few visited the synagogue also. So both shared their fears, ate and prayed together. As he was leaving, the rabbi expressed his sorrow at not being able to give the abbot the help he wanted, but commented at their parting that one of them at the monastery was the Messiah!

On his return to the monastery, the Abbot relayed what had occurred to the other monks, adding the very puzzling statement about the rabbi declaring that one of them was the Messiah. In the days, weeks and months that passed, the old monks thought long and hard about this strange message. The Messiah is one of us? Which one? Could it be the Abbot? He had been in charge for a long time and was a very devout man. On the other hand, Brother Thomas was so holy, he was always in prayer and contemplation. Or Brother Eldred, he seems to be always right. What about Brother Philip, so peaceful and kind, always at hand to help? And each even thought about himself, could he be the Messiah? As an ordinary monk, each tried his best, but to be the Messiah, surely not!

As they contemplated in this manner, the old monks began to treat each other with extraordinary respect on the offchance that one among them might be the Messiah. This aura of tremendous respect that began to surround the old monks seemed to radiate out from and permeate the atmosphere of the place. There was something strangely compelling and attractive about the place. Hardly knowing why, many visitors started to come to the old monastery and its beautiful grounds, to picnic, to play, to pray. They began to tell their friends, and they brought others to this special place.

Then it happened that some of the younger men who came started to talk more and more with the old monks. After a while one asked if he could join, then another, and another. So within a few years the monastery had once again become a thriving order and a vibrant centre of light and spirituality, all thanks to the rabbi's gift.

7 Path of empowerment

By recognising and using our soul qualities, we activate our incredible spiritual potential, things then move, work and come together, pulling anything dysfunctional and discordant into its harmonic wavelength. Whatever has gone wrong, failed or become negative can now be restored, regenerated and empowered. Soul consciousness becomes the catalyst for success and fulfilment. Just turn the key of self-awareness and the fountain of pure consciousness cascades into our open and receptive mind.

This quantum movement, from body centredness into soul awareness, enables us to make the great leap into control, power and change. Here we are able to stabilise our mind in the permanency of our original, spiritual form and qualities. In doing so, we can then let go of the props and supports that we have long surrounded ourselves with. We now move into an arena of freedom and growth, where we not only make sense of our fast changing world, but in discovering our true spiritual potential, we are able to be completely self sustaining.

As we begin to find and free ourselves, we can, as a result, stand back from blinkered self obsession and begin to truly appreciate and have genuine good wishes for what others are trying to do and achieve, as they too wrestle with the self same quandaries and paradoxes of their own particular life journey.

So let us take these ideas and use them as part of our next reflection.

Meditation

Internalising my awareness,
I let go of the self-centredness of my prevailing world
and I open my self to a natural and pure benevolence,
where I can understand, relate and give support
to the world of my brothers.
I can now help others
through my attitude and thoughts of good wishes and pure
     feelings.
I help others by abandoning my critical mind and judgmental
     vision.
I help others by allowing my heart to beat with their heart,
to walk in their shoes,
to see with their eyes.
I help others by dancing the dance of harmony,
moving as they move
and appreciating their role,
their effort and their speciality.
I help others when I play my part,
not another's;
and in this,
I'm left to focus on what I need to know
and what I need to do.
And I realise that through vibrations of love,
brotherhood and unlimited compassion,
I help myself by helping others.
It is through this giving,
this sharing,
that I grow.
And my heart becomes full and loving.

8 Path of happiness

Without food, our bodies would certainly fail; but what of our soul, what food do we give? Or is it continually in a state of hunger and malnourishment? What is it, more than anything, that we hunger and yearn for? Isn't it happiness and fulfilment? Yet, how scarce is this commodity in the markets of the world!

But as Epictetus the Roman philosopher said;
"There is only one way to happiness and that is to cease worrying about things which are beyond the power of our will."

It is certainly true that when we go into any form of extension outside ourselves and beyond our control, we become vulnerable and liable to all sorts of influence and effects. So the great secret of happiness lies in focussing on areas that concern only ourselves, as Ken Keyes puts it;

"There's only one person in the world that can really make you happy.
There's only one person in the world that can really make you unhappy.
How about getting to know this person more deeply?
For a starter, go look in the mirror and smile and say, "Hello".
And then tell yourself that for a while you're going to quit putting so much energy into trying to change the people around you. It hasn't worked that well, has it? Instead, you're going to put your energy into the inner work on your own mind that will enable you to use the prescriptions for happiness skilfully and effectively in your daily life."

(*PATHWAYS TO HIGHER CONSCIOUSNESS*)

So what is the prescription for happiness? Well, the following ten principles will certainly, if practised, take you a long way along that path to attaining and living a life that is carefree and happy.

Ten principles to experience happiness

Instructions
Take each of the following points and think deeply about what it means to you personally.
See yourself using that.
How do you feel?
See how others also benefit.

(**Become a child and a master**)

When you speak and act, be a master, one who has the aim of not giving sorrow. In doing so you fulfil your responsibility to address the issue and situation. But then let go and become the child. In the consciousness of the child, there is acceptance, openness and trustfulness. As a child there is a feeling of being carefree that precludes any worry or stress, enabling the mind to fully experience and enjoy the present moment.

And to see the world with a child's eye, as Einstein reminds us;

> "There are only two ways to live your life. One is as though nothing is a miracle. The other is as though everything is a miracle."

> "I am, I have always been and I will always be
> God's child.
> Never doubt this.
> There is such strength in this experience. You will easily rise above adversity. Sorrow will finish and your heart will dance. Belonging to God fills you with the innocence of a child and the wisdom of God."

> DADI JANKI, *COMPANION OF GOD*

Silence

Is when we slip into our inner world away from the noise and the demands and needs of our chaotic world. Where our mind free falls into a subtle world of light and pure energy, to float in a sea of calm and soft serenity. Have these moments of silence throughout the day. It's by controlling and focusing the mind that we gain control over our wayward thought patterns. Then as thoughts slow down, we will start to make sense of things. With this clarity we start to break our old patterns of negative thought, which regularly plunder our present happiness. So now, stop pitching about on the high seas of projection, but slip into the enclosed bay of the inner mind and experience the calm waters of stability and peace.

> "Silence allows you to manage your thoughts better. You will find, for example, that there is no need to think as much as you do, that simply sitting in silence will emerge, effortlessly, much of all that you need. Silence releases you from the grip of your negative programming and conditioning. You will more easily experience the truth of your inner peace and dignity. This further aids the mind in remaining focused and capable."
>
> DADI JANKI, *COMPANION OF GOD*

See life as a play

As Shakespeare said, "All the world's a stage, and all the men and women merely actors, they have their exits and their entrances, and one man in his time plays many parts."
I now understand that each soul is interpreting their part as best as they can according to the influence and conditioning of their past and according to their present consciousness. I cannot play or truly understand their part, nor they mine. So let me just concentrate on what I have to do and do it well and not invade their space. Let me appreciate that what each one does, is only their part in the great play of life, but they are not their part. For like me, they are unique, spiritual beings on the journey to fulfilment. Through this awareness, I become free and content.

> And as for life, says Paramahansa Yogananda,
> "Do not take life's experiences too seriously. Above all, do not let them hurt you, for in reality they are nothing but experiences

... If circumstances are bad and you have to bear them, do not make them part of yourself. Play your part in life, but never forget that it is only a role."

Don't give sorrow or accept sorrow

Realising my own true spiritual nature, I do not allow external influences to dictate my experience. I am not dependent on others or on circumstances. I now create my own experiential world through the awareness of being soul conscious. I now live in the light and my nature is to spread that light. To give hurt to another is to hurt myself, for we are all one in the family of love. Remember,

"To be upset over what you don't have ... is to waste what you do have."

KEN KEYES

Laugh

Learn to see the funny side of things. This really helps to diffuse anger and upsets, and relieves tension and fear. Laughter gives us space before we react. In that space, things change, resolve; we change and can move on. It stops us becoming pompous and egotistical. We feel good. When we laugh, the world will laugh too.

"Be a fundamentalist – make sure the *fun* always comes before the *mental*. Life is a situation comedy and a laugh track has been provided. Have a good laughsitive twice a day, and that will ensure regular-hilarity."

Give, give and give

Whatever we do, we automatically experience the return, whether it's smiling, giving a helping hand, or a word of wisdom. What seems to be missing from our life and from our relationships, is whatever we haven't given. Whatever we desire, be it respect, love, co-operation or happiness, we have to give it first ourselves for it then to come to us. Giving is about allowing others to have space, time, a chance, it's about acceptance, empathy, listening, it's about being honest, yet non-critical. As a result of giving, our heart grows big and we move into the unlimited, supported by the blessings of others. So each day give a gift to yourself of one virtue or quality, and allow that garden to grow and produce the fruits of happiness.

> "To hate another is to hate yourself. We all live within the one Universal Mind. What we think about another, we think about ourselves. If you have an enemy, forgive him now. Let all bitterness and resentment dissolve ... Show charity and goodwill toward others and it will return to enhance your own life in many wonderful ways."
>
> BRIAN ADAMS

Think deeply – contemplate

When we are in silence, tapping into our creative heart centre, then we are thinking deeply over things, pondering their depth, connections and significance. This will create new awareness, wisdom and creativity. Each time, these new realizations produce fresh mindsets that bring insight and enthusiasm, so helping to move away the blocks and barriers of the past, thus giving rise to a greater sense and feeling of confidence and growth.

As Rajneesh advises when we have a problem:
> "Just stand aside and look at the problem. Is it really there? Or have you created it? Look deeply into it, and you will suddenly see it is not increasing. It is decreasing; it is becoming smaller and smaller. The more you put your energy into observation, the smaller it becomes. And a moment comes when suddenly it is not there ... you will have a good laugh."

See benefit in everything

See everything as a play, then each scene, each role is correct and accurate. Change brings newness and renewal. Whatever has happened let me learn from that; what new significance can I draw. The old often has to be dismantled before the new can be created. Accept what has happened. Let it go. Build on that. Move into the now and be happy. The Chinese characters for "crisis" are danger or opportunity; we always have the choice to take the positive track and so travel on towards our goal.

Accept yourself

I am a loving, aware and powerful soul, who is accepted and loved by all. I am unique, there is nobody on the planet like me. I have come to play a very special role. Soul consciousness moves us naturally away from comparison and jealousy, creating an experiential world where we have the opportunity to enjoy and appreciate not only our own role and specialities but also those of others. And also knowing that God loves us we become free, light and carefree.

> "The moment you accept yourself as you are, all the burdens, all mountainous burdens, simply disappear. Then life is a sheer joy, a festival of lights."
>
> SHRI RAJNEESH

Make God your strength

Linking into God's light and power can bring fast change and empowerment. The subtle effects of the past can be lifted and all tasks shared. Everything starts to become easy. Talk to God. Listen to God. Share with God. Touchings, inspirations and ways forward start to emerge. In this happiness, the heart is lifted beyond into a joyous acceptance of all things; and such is the feeling of harmony, that everything feels at that moment as one, nothing is seen as separate, everything is felt as part of the soul's holistic world, leaving a wonderful feeling of all-encompassing love.

As we reflect on these ten points let us use them as a means to deepen our awareness.

9 Path to God

Just as when the body becomes overworked and run down and the remedy is to get medicine from a doctor or go on a detox diet, our soul also at times needs an injection, an input of new energy, to recreate enthusiasm, to enable it to move effectively along life's path.

As nature revives itself with the coming of the rejuvenating sun, so it has long been remembered in scriptures, myths and fables that newness and change come through the intervention of God's power.

As mankind has gradually slipped into spiritual amnesia due to wrong awareness and association, so the connection and belief in God has also weakened.

Spirituality is about recalling what has been lost and what has been forgotten.

For a long time, the two main parts of our metaphysical jigsaw have been out of alignment or just simply lost, resulting in a great deal of confusion. Debate and counter-debate on the nature of the self and who in fact is God, have long perplexed our philosophical minds, leaving most of us none the wiser.

An exercise that may help resolve our confusion is for us to sit in the laboratory of the mind, using the discernment of a clear and peaceful intellect, and ask the following:

- ▶ Who am I? What role(s) do I play?
- ▶ What is it that I need on my journey and in my relationships for them to be successful?
- ▶ Where is it I want to go? A place of peace or of perfection?
- ▶ What is the nature and qualities of God? How near am I to these?

▸ What is His role? Do I play any of these?

▸ What is God's relationship to me?

Ponder these questions yourself and come to your own conclusions.

Coming close to God

To achieve this, we need three things;

1 **Faith in His existence**; a belief that He is a reality, a consciousness, playing an active, guiding role in the affairs of mankind.

2 **An understanding of our spiritual reality**; that I am not just the physical body, but my spiritual self is the energy and consciousness that works through my body, that shapes my decisions and relates to the world.

3 **A desire to come close and know God**; knowing that through this connection my soul will receive support, power and transformation.

We then create a platform and springboard to transcend the physical dimension. Through this subtle positioning, we can now move directly into the orbit and influence of God the Supreme and so take power directly.

This coming together with the Supreme Soul is the peak point of our meditation experience. Our earlier spiritual efforts have been like rungs on the ladder, each step taking us closer to this ultimate experience. Now we can access the highest and purest form of spiritual energy.

To experience this, we first need to focus our awareness on the form of the Supreme Soul. Let us see that form as a radiant point of love, light energy that is unlimited and full of unlimited love and compassion. Holding this in our consciousness we are ready to move into a meditation of union.

Meditation

From the centred focus of my own self awareness,
I now let go of the influence of my body and of the surrounding
    world.
With my thoughts I can travel beyond,
and go to the world of subtle light.
Here I find myself in the presence of the Supreme Soul,
the Supreme Energy.
I focus and centre my attention on His form of light.
Concentrating,
going closer and deeper into this pure being of love.
I stay fixed,
held by that incredible power and vibration,
experiencing union,
a fusion of energies, feelings,
of thoughts becoming no thought,
of minds becoming like one mind.
There is stillness,
oneness.
And slowly,
emphatically,
the effects of the past,
the hurts and pain of old memory,
begin to diminish and finish,
as the healing light of God's pure love,
bathes and soothes and heals.
I am refreshed,
renewed,
rejuvenated.

Go slowly over each line and allow its significance to fill your awareness. If you find your mind wavering or wandering whilst thinking on the Supreme, have patience and gently bring your mind back to that focus and allow the experience to take hold.

10 Path of the hero

Ancient journeys

Since the early dawn of man's struggle to make some sense of his life and his purpose, he has made use of simple tales and powerful epics which are full of noble deeds and heroic figures; symbols, analogies, representations of particular wisdoms, truths and understandings, all used to guide us on our journey into awareness.

Yet, strangely, since the appearance of these legends, we are certainly left with stories and images, yet, often, the true meaning and intention has been lost or simply just forgotten, as a result of which there occurs, as Joseph Campbell says "A misinterpretation of mythology... which consists precisely in attributing historical references to symbols which properly are spiritual in their reference."

Such authorities as Jung and Campbell tended to see myths as allegories for inner processes of spiritual transformation, that is, as stories that are symbolic, not actually true.

The ancients' symbolical treatment of universal human longings, fears and aspirations serves as a guide to our present experiences by making the contents of the personal and collective unconscious accessible through symbology and the vehicle of the hero.

In many of the epics and legends, a desire to move out and away and discover a higher and greater truth, or a magical, healing talisman, or to find a new and wondrous world were all very common themes, which I believe are analogies of a deeper and more profound spiritual journey – the journey of the soul in its search for spiritual experience and fulfilment.

In almost every culture and belief system are found tales of heroes and noble beings who go in search of new life, experience and truth – Odysseus, Jason and the Argonauts, The Arthurian Knights of the Round Table and so on.

As Campbell and Mircieu have shown, there is possibly really only one story, translated in the traditions and circumstances of a myriad people. It is the myth of the lost idyllic "Time of Beginning", and of a hero's journey to restore the world to its pristine condition of "paradisal splendour" .

It's interesting to note that there are various common threads to be found in those who take on these journeys.

- Those who go on a search or quest are heroic and noble or as a result become noble.
- They have to be renunciates, i.e. they have to let go of their present world in order to pursue their goal, which is in itself elevated, worthy and heroic.
- Whilst overcoming difficulties through tests and trials, they develop wisdom and awareness.
- Those who succeed are those who obey their truth.
- Those who follow the laws are protected and victorious.
- Those who reach their goal never lose or forget their aim and purpose.
- Success comes when they use or take the help of a higher power or God.

These heroic journeys are memories of our own spiritual journey, memories of how we try to make sense of who we are, what we need to do and ultimately, where we need to reach.

The journeys of the heroes are our journeys.

Their journey is our journey.

Their trials are our trials.

Their triumphs are our triumphs.

We are those heroes!

Thus we need to harness their wisdom, their courage, their focus and determination.

We can do this through a reflection on our own life's journey.

Meditation

I turn away
and let go of the surrounding worlds
of desire, ego and accumulation.
For now my purpose,
my focus
is to return to truth,
to the way of harmony,
to the form of my perfection.
Turning within,
I slip into the dimension of silence,
into the inner world of subtle light.
My thoughts and energies begin to slow.
There is a great feeling of calmness and serenity.
And I am drawn towards and begin to experience
those subtle, soft energies of the spiritual self.
Centring my thoughts
on the love, light energy
of my soul light form,
I begin to stir the river bed of my true, pure consciousness
and like a beautiful fountain.
I begin to emerge my natural energies
of peace and love and light,
which begin to move and flow
and fill my being with its healing power.
As that love and light and peace flows
in and around me,
I am refreshed
and restored.
The wounds and the hurts of the past
begin to fade and are no more.
I have now moved into the light
and I am empowered.

From this inner place,
this inner state,
I see around me the world of action
and of natural forms.
I see those in pain.
I see those who are hungry,
who cry out
and who are overwhelmed
by the waves of fear and sorrow.
Yet, on my journey into light,
to meet those needs,
I send good wishes and purest thought;
my vibrations, thoughts, my words,
are full of upliftment and deepest compassion.
In my soul-conscious state,
I watch the scenes of anguish and of confusion,
I am the detached observer,
uninfluenced and unaffected.
I now can help with understanding and with mercy.
And I move on,
not ignoring,
not stopping,
but embracing all.
I see the illusions,
the false and empty words
and all the crumbling systems of our world.
Yet, I let them go.
I see also,
the actors and the actions,
in life's great play.
I see with eyes of understanding and appreciation.
Each interpreting their part as best they can,
according to their understanding
and the conditioning of their nature.

I watch and see with mercy and good wishes.
And I travel on,
and whoever I meet on the journey of life,
I try to give them whatever they need,
give what is best for them.
And from all that I see
and in all that I experience,
I learn.
I grow in awareness and in love.
I use the touchstone of knowledge
and spiritual truth to guide my thoughts,
to guide my journey.
And as I travel,
my light grows strong,
my heart expands.
And I move closer to the centre
of God's true light.

11 Path of transformation

In today's world, with the loss of spiritual identity, there has been for many a loss of power, direction and hope. Often, there are times, being surrounded by seemingly insurmountable problems and pressures, when the question of any sort of personal change can be seen as extremely difficult, if not impossible.

With inner resolve and strength diminishing and with science and technology increasing, it has been all too easy to become completely dependent on others and the creations of technology.

However, spirituality reveals to us secrets and laws that have been ignored by many and forgotten by most.

It tells us that the mechanism for change lies not with the prevailing gods of science and technology; but in fact, in the power of individual consciousness.

Spiritual consciousness is about being nurtured and sustained by metaphysical rather than physical processes. It's about living and experiencing a life centred on the well spring of the soul's original nature and guided by God's pure energy.

Change comes when we decide to invoke and channel spiritual energy from the Supreme into the armoury of our own awareness. So empowered, we then have the strength to let go of the past and create a whole new pattern of powerful and meaningful behaviour and activity.

The Experience of God

"There is a lot of light coming to us from God; a light which is not of a physical nature. It touches our intellect, opening a lock on our awareness. And we find ourselves again receptive to all God's powers – like peace and love. These again start filling the soul. And the feeling is of having found something precious that we had somehow lost."

DADI JANKI *WINGS OF THE SOUL*

Our link with the Supreme acts like a huge magnet drawing us deep into God's unlimited Ocean, an experience that becomes the key to unlock our soul's internal treasure store. This connection with the Supreme is the catalyst through which the mainly unknown and untapped world of our inner being emerges and becomes available to our conscious mind.

To come into the experience of God's pure energy, we first need to have the understanding of the Supreme as a being of pure, light energy, who is resident in the golden, silent realm beyond the dimensions of matter; then we can focus our thoughts on His form of power and His form of light. Our mind can then be held and stabilised in that incredible force field of unlimited consciousness.In this focused union, the powerful energy of the Supreme activates and recharges our soul energy, taking us to the highest state of empowerment and spiritual awareness. So now with this understanding, let us transcend the physical world and fly to the region of silent light, to unite with the love energy of God the Supreme.

Meditation

Centred in self awareness,
feeling light,
full of light,
I move effortlessly beyond all limitations,
beyond the pulls of this earthly world
and move into the awareness
and company of the Supreme,
whose radiant form
holds me in its awesome beauty.
Slowly, I am drawn closer,

deeper,
it's as if I'm becoming merged
in that pure energy field of highest experience –
The Supreme,
the unlimited ocean of purest love –
and I go deep into that love,
I experience that love
I am that love.
I allow myself to stay absorbed,
centred in that love
there is nothing but love.
I am love.

Using this meditation on a regular basis provides you with a vehicle that can help bring about a great deal of personal change. Give time in the early hours before work and again in the early evening and your meditation will develop strongly and become very powerful.

In this state of God awareness, it becomes a lot easier to let go and become free of our obsessions, fears and negative desires, and we then are able to move into a more unlimited state of awareness, where we start to see more clearly fresh alternatives, new patterns and the wider significance of our actions. Through this awakening, we gain the ability and strength to transform our weaknesses and overcome obstacles, so taking us one more step further along the way of true love.

Reconciling the past

As we connect with our present day world, our plans and progress are often interfered with and disrupted by negative effects from our past. These come in such forms as mental or physical ill health, negative habits, lack of awareness and judgement and the numerous forms of anxiety and stress, to our involvement with the huge upheavals in the physical world. All these aspects are recorded and held in the grooves of our subconscious personality and become ready to emerge and play out their setting at the appropriate time.

The role of meditation

Through meditation, we have the ability to avoid many of these repercussions. Just as we have programmed our present and future by our actions in the past, we can, in the same way, now spiritually re-programme ourselves through soul-conscious and God-conscious awareness. Perceptions and awareness will switch onto such an effective, transformative level that they will completely alter the previous patterns laid down.

It is in this affirmative reassertion of the soul's original nature over the illusory state of body consciousness that we begin to create a new and powerful pattern of positive spiritual activity. This re-structuring of consciousness automatically supersedes the old systems of action, which when no longer used, loses influence and effect, and in time gradually diminishes and disappears.

It's interesting to note that the innovative world is spending billions on techniques and products, attempting renovation, change and newness, (with, it seems little success), yet, here just simply with a little understanding and a re-focusing of awareness, many of our needs can be met.

Benefits of God awareness

In our meditation, the pure vibration of the Supreme brings about a two-fold transformational effect. First, there occurs a spiritual synchronicity, a becoming as one, as the soul is drawn into the harmony of God's still centre, bringing healing, hope and a new resolve.

Secondly, there occurs a massive shift in the internal structure of the soul, just as when spring breaks through the heavy hold of winter and new life comes. So also, like a beautiful fountain, the natural, spiritual force of the soul stirs, activates and floods our consciousness.

As a result, the effects of the past are displaced, replaced and resolved, and the soul moves into a state of purity, power and awareness. The mind now firmly rooted in the present can begin to focus, think clearly and function effectively. Our attitude, now empowered by the Supreme, becomes one of positivity, benevolence and compassion, so giving rise to words and actions full of purpose, sweetness and love.

With this understanding, let us experience this powerful state of God awareness.

Meditation

In the form of light of the original self,
I lift away from the heaviness of this physical world
and travel to the world of light.
Here I come into connection with the Supreme,
whose unlimited love
surrounds and envelops me
and draws me to His centre.
Although thoughts, habits and influences of the physical world
pull and cajole me to return,
I'm held,
supported in the stillness of His perfect form,
and through this deep union with the Supreme,
I am nurtured,
I grow strong,
for here I am in the heart centre of unlimited love,
such love
which enables me to let go of my accumulated sorrows
and heal the scars and traumas of the past.
I can now let all these go
and become free,
free and full of love,
a love which grows and blossoms
into a fire of purest love,
whose joy, intensity and wondrous beauty
surrounds me,
fills me.
There is nothing but love,
love and more love.

12 Path of relationship

On our great and epic spiritual journey, it has been our individual nature and individual needs that have determined our aspirations and activity. Central to these needs has been the desire for someone to share our journey, to walk, to care, to share our sorrows and our joys. Someone to be our parent, friend, helper, lover and teacher. All these have been the source of our greatest joys, yet, when they fail – the source of our greatest sorrows.

Now linking with the Supreme, we shift from the limited to the unlimited. We can move into a relationship with a being who is totally accepting, compassionate, unwavering, benevolent and totally altruistic.

The process of relationship

As in most relationships, it takes time to come close and really know and accept the other. There is first the initial coming together, introduction and period of meetings and polite conversation. It is a time where there is a kind of stand-off, seeing where the other is at: Do I like this person? Do they like me? Gradually, as more things are recognised and understood, the relationship deepens, acceptance and appreciation comes in.

With our new-found relationship, we can walk the path together – connecting, experiencing, sharing the needs of the everyday world. As a result things become easier and we become closer. Slowly, a more relaxed atmosphere emerges, as closeness and love begins to blossom. It is so with God.

But maybe we are still struggling with the concept of a Divine

Being, or the very word God itself? Yet, it's interesting to speculate that most of our reactions, rejections and hesitant feelings probably come from experiences of a hurt or confused past; and so now we limp into the present with all sorts of spiritual disabilities and fragmented outlooks.

So we first need to go through a gentle process of healing and reconciliation – a period of discovery, of coming together, talking, sharing and developing trust. The first steps in our meditation will be built on this, introducing ourselves and getting to understand and know better God the Supreme, the source and the centre of unlimited love.

Meditation

Adopting the awareness and form of light,
I the soul,
slip away from my physical costume
and travel beyond the material world
to the unlimited dimension of purest light.
In this world of freedom and unlimited peace,
I come into connection
with the form of the Supreme Soul,
a beautiful light
of purest energy and consciousness.
I move towards that form of light.
I focus my thoughts and awareness on the Supreme.
The Ocean of unlimited love.
I go deep into that love,
I experience that love,
and I become that love.
The Supreme is the Ocean of peace,
I go deep into that peace,
and I experience that peace
and I become that peace.
Stabilised and absorbed in this experience,

there are now no thoughts of worry or fear.
I enjoy this freedom
within which
I feel accepted, loved and empowered.
I can share the feelings of my heart,
share my dreams and aspirations
with One who I know really understands me,
believes in me
and can powerfully help me to achieve my deepest desires.

Knowing God

Through the vehicle of meditation, we are pulled into the orbit of the attraction and spiritual power of the Supreme. Consequently, as this experience increases, it's then natural for us to want to deepen these feelings and develop a much closer relationship.

Though the Supreme Soul is not physical and has no physical emotions, physical relationships or personality traits, it is by using physical analogy and symbolism that we can unravel and access much of the mystery of God's pure consciousness. These resonating symbols can take us deep into our subconscious and God-conscious nature, bringing us to a more profound understanding and spiritual realization.

In the myriad cultures and belief systems of our world, there are so many symbols and forms already used to explain and relate to God, such as trees, rivers, mountains, animals, buildings, people, as well as the numerous composite forms drawn from man's intricate mind. Yet, through time, ironically, we can observe that it is God who has generally been forgotten, leaving only the symbol, usually to be revered or worshipped.

Although we can still use these symbols to build a more intimate and profound relationship with God, we need to focus on more emotive and personal forms. One way is to use relationships that we have had or desire to have had, like mother, friend or teacher, and to transfer these to the Supreme. In this way, we create an avenue of least resistance and difficulty to the understanding and experience of God.

The parent

One of our greatest needs is to love, and be loved. By taking God as our parent we open ourselves to the purest and deepest love connection of all. As our mother, the Supreme draws us deep into her lap of compassionate mercy and unconditional love. As our father, he gives us the strength and support to cope with things that become difficult and dangerous. So with the Supreme as our Divine Parent we move under a canopy of protective love where we begin to feel safe and secure, enabling us to grow in confidence and self esteem.

Let us bring these ideas into meditation.

Meditation

With the thought of love,
I adopt the consciousness of the spiritual child
I let go of my adult ego,
I let go of the form and role of my body
and I now become a child of the Supreme.
The Supreme,
my Mother,
who has always known and loved me,
now places me in her heart,
the centre of her overflowing love.
I am enfolded and protected
in the lap of care, compassion and mercy,
I feel so free,
safe, light,
and so loved.
Here nothing can influence me,
nothing can hurt me,
for I am with my unlimited,
Beloved Mother.
The Supreme as my Father,
also knows me,

loves me
and accepts me as I am,
for who I am.
I feel and accept
that I am His beloved child,
who sits in His heart
and in His eyes,
He is the one who gives me support and power
and clear guidance for all that I do.
In this company of my Divine Parent,
I can never feel alone or sad,
or feel I have to face
the trials and tests of life's long journey by myself,
for the Supreme,
my parent, is constantly with me.
And now in this beautiful unity,
focusing on the light,
loveful form of the Supreme,
I can,
for a few moments,
confide my thoughts and dreams.
Knowing that what I think and say and feel,
is accepted and understood,
and that my Divine Parent will give me
the necessary support and strength and guidance.

The friend

A true friend is one with whom you can share your joys, secrets and greatest fears. Someone who accepts you unconditionally and who connects on a level of equality and respect. God as our friend is all these.

For the heart of the Supreme Soul is full and overflowing, constantly reassuring, giving us unconditional support, confidence and strength.

With such a friend, can we ever again feel that we stand alone against the circumstances of the world?

With God as our friend, the heaviness of the past and the difficulties of the present are soon forgotten in the happiness and joy of this special relationship. Whatever comes, we stand together, combined – and everything becomes easy.

Meditation

With the thought of love,
in the form of love,
I travel to the world of love,
to the source of love,
to the form and being of the Supreme,
the Ocean of unlimited love,
my dear, close friend.
We greet each other with a familiar feeling of closeness,
respect and deep friendship.
Here with my sweet, unlimited friend,
I feel harmonious,
as a warm contentedness pervades me.
I can share my thoughts and deepest feelings,
unload any worries or perplexing thoughts,
knowing that the Supreme,
my true friend, understands and totally accepts me,
as I am, for what I am.
I feel a great thankfulness and love.
In this close state of unity,
I can share the feelings of my heart,
my secrets and my plans.
Here too, I smile and laugh,
I laugh at life,
I laugh at death
and at all the things I thought so important

and realise that it is just a game,
a game for us to enjoy.

In resurrecting our eternal relationship with the Supreme, our heart and mind becomes filled with His energy and presence, and as a result, things start to dramatically change. The emptiness and the confusions gradually become settled and resolved and the challenges that formerly seemed so daunting now no longer hold a threat.

With such support, we become empowered by a renewed faith and confidence, knowing that we now no longer walk alone, but each step is now filled with God's power and support.

13   Path of benevolence

Through our meditation experiences, we gradually grow strong and confident. However, as our own inner world begins to transform and grow brighter, the external conditions of strife, deprivation, exploitation and inequality certainly remain and in many instances grow worse.

Often, through the media, we hear of or witness traumatic happenings, like earthquakes, floods, brutalities or wars. Not only are we horrified, also, because of magnitude and distance, we can often feel helpless and inadequate.

Through meditation, we can step into a dimension of pure thought, into an eternal, timeless present. Here in the same moment, we can be connected with all souls. Our consciousness transforms and connects into a universal matrix of energy systems that are linked and tuned into all things. And from here we can give support and hope and inspiration through our subtle presence, or we can direct pure and powerful thought along these subtle energy channels, to the hearts and minds of many souls.

As we centre our mind in the heart throne of God's love, we become a means, a channel to release light into our world, uplifting, healing and restoring the animal kingdoms and the natural and physical worlds.

This spiritual energy not only helps souls move into a more positive state of hope and determination, but more importantly, is a means to help revive the soul's memory and relationship with God.

Linked with One, let us now send these vibrations out into the world. To help with this practice, you might find it useful to bring the image of the earth in front of yourself and see it being surrounded by these powerful energies. If you wish, you may like to highlight a particular area of our planet that needs help at this time:

Meditation

In the awareness of my eternal
and original nature of the soul,
I unite my consciousness with the Supreme,
the unlimited ocean of purest energy and understanding;
in this combined form
of soul and the Supreme Soul,
I become centred,
as one,
experiencing the benevolent nature of God.
And in this most elevated state of love,
I turn my attention towards the Earth,
where heavy clouds now surround
and hide its beauty
and many storms rage in people's hearts,
so from this the heart centre of the Supreme,
I send to my brothers and sisters,
vibrations and waves
of pure good feeling and spiritual help,
to touch,
uplift
and help move forward,
creating such light
that they may see
and so find their way out and away
from their fears and illusions,
so sowing the seeds
of hope and love and truth.

Conclusion

Meditation is the pathway that enables us to let go of the old. It is the energy that revives and regenerates our tiredness, our hope and our will. It teaches us not only to begin to love ourselves, but opens our heart centre to the world around. This inner journey is one of self-discovery, a means to access our own spiritual treasures, which become stepping stones to the immense powers of God. This union of the soul and God is the key to personal change. It's a fantastic empowerment through which the purest spiritual energy floods the soul's core centre, healing and reconciling the past, focussing the vision on that which is important in the present and preparing the soul to move to a future that is assured and benevolent.

For myself, meditation has given me a wonderful sense of purpose; a clarity to understand what was going on inside my head, to make sense of all the emotional swirl that was sloshing around. It helped me to channel all these feelings into avenues of creativity and usefulness. It also helped me for the first time to think rationally about issues and circumstances, and make some sort of sense of our often chaotic and confusing world.

As my link and relationship with the Supreme grew through my meditations, it developed in me an amazing feeling of freedom and lightness; what was there to worry about, what more did I need?

Having read this little book, I trust that you too will also experience some of these benefits and use them as another stepping stone into the vast world of spiritual truth, for this is only the first of many doors that await your entry.

Bibliography

Christina Feldman and Jack Kornfield, *Stories of the Spirit, Stories of the Heart*, HarperCollins, London, 1991

Susan Hayward, *A Guide for the Advanced Soul*, Little Brown and Company, London, 1984

Richard Heinberg, *Memories and Visions of Paradise*, Aquarian Press, London, 1990

Ken Keyes Jr., *Prescriptions For Happiness*, Love Line Books, Oregon, USA, 1985

Dadi Janki, *Wings of the Soul*, Health Communications, Inc., Deerfield Beach, Fla, USA, 1998

Dadi Janki, *Companion of God*, Brahma Kumaris Spiritual University Pub., London, 1996

In the Light of Meditation
Mike George

In the Light of Meditation offers an introduction to the art and practice of meditation while laying down the foundations for ongoing spiritual development. A series of ten lessons provide specific insights into Raja Yoga, with practical exercises to complement and to help your understanding of the method and underlying teachings.

Accessible, powerful and challenging, this book shows how meditation is more an experience than something that you do, more a process than an achievement, more an ongoing inner journey than a destination. Take your time, be patient with yourself and always be ready to go back to basics, to lesson one, the true identity of the self, which is the foundation of everything.

Beautifully illustrated in full colour, it comes with a CD.

Mike George is a spiritual teacher, motivational speaker, retreat leader and management development facilitator. He brings together the three key strands of his millennium-spiritual and emotional intelligence, leadership development, and continuous learning. His previous books include *Discover Inner Peace, Learn to Relax* and *The 7 Aha!s.*

1 905047 72 X

The 7 Aha!s of Highly Enlightened Souls
Mike George

With thousands of insights now flooding the market place of spiritual development, how do we begin to decide where to start our spiritual journey? What are the right methods? This book strips away the illusions that surround the modern malaise we call stress. In 7 insights, it reminds us of the essence of all the different paths of spiritual wisdom. It succinctly describes what we need to realize in order to create authentic happiness and live with greater contentment. It finishes with the 7 AHA!S, the "eureka moments", the practice of any one of which will profoundly change your life in the most positive way.

Mike George is a spiritual teacher, motivational speaker, retreat leader and management development facilitator. He brings together the three key strands of his millennium-spiritual and emotional intelligence, leadership development, and continuous learning. His previous books include *Discover Inner Peace, Learn to Relax* and *In The Light of Meditation*.

1 903816 31 9
£5.99/$11.95

Relax Kids: Aladdin's Magic Carpet
52 magical meditations for princesses and superheroes
Marneta Viegas

Using guided meditations based around traditional stories this is a gentle and fun way of introducing older children to the world of meditation and relaxation. It is designed to counteract some of the tensions with which we are all familiar at the end of a busy day, and offer parent and children together some quality time to relax and share.

"Enchanting! This book deserves to sit by the bedside of every child (and adult too!). Every page is brimming with imagination, creativity and positivity." Robert Holden, founder of The Happiness Project and author

Marneta Viegas has run her own children's entertainment business for 10 years, and

has appeared at venues ranging from Buckingham Palace to working with street children in India.

1 903816 66 1
£9.95/$14.95

Soul Power
Nikki de Carteret

How do you create inner stability in times of chaos? How do you cultivate the power of presence? Where does humility meet mastery? These are just some of the threads of spiritual inquiry that Nikki weaves into a tapestry of Soul Power. Juxtaposing fascinating teachings from the ancient mystics with stories of modern seekers, as well as her own extraordinary journey towards wholeness, she invites you to explore the factors that drain your spiritual energy, and what transformational forces restore it.

I have, quite simply, never before read a book that made me feel so keenly the love of God. Joy Parker, author of *Woman Who Glows in the Dark.*

A beautiful and touching expression of the spiritual journey. Barbara Shipka, author of *Leadership in a Challenging World.*

A unique combination of scholarly research and hands-on experience. Michael Rymer, Hollywood film director

Nikki de Carteret holds a master's degree from the Sorbonne in medieval mystic literature and leads workshops around the world on personal and organizational transformation.

1 903816 17 3
£9.99/$14.95

Everyday Buddha
A contemporary rendering of the Buddhist classic,
The Dhammapada
Karma Yonten Senge

These quintessential sayings of the Buddha offer a rich tapestry of spiritual teachings and reflections on the spiritual path. More than just a collection of Buddhist sayings, *The Dhammapada's* message is timeless and crosses all cultural boundaries. It offers the reader a constant source of inspiration, reflection and companionship. It is a treasure trove of pure wisdom that has something to offer to everyone.

Everyday Buddha brings the original teaching and traditional text of *The Dhammapada* into our 21st century lifestyle, with a contemporary context. Without straying far from the Pali text it renders it in a fresh and modern idiom, with a universal appeal. An introduction provides a background to the life and times of the historical Buddha, and his teachings on the four noble truths and eight fold noble path.

Foreword by H.H. The Dalai Lama, with his seal of approval.

Karma Yonten Senge is a Dharma practitioner of the Karma Kagyu tradition of Tibetan Buddhism. He is an avid follower of Buddha Dharma, and currently lives in Australia.

1 905047 30 4
£9.99/$19.95

The Ocean of Wisdom

Alan Jacobs

The most comprehensive anthology of spiritual wisdom available

The first major anthology of this size and scope since 1935, *The Ocean of Wisdom* collects over five thousand pearls in poetry and prose, from the earliest of recorded history to modern times. Divided into 54 sections, ranging from Action to Zen, it draws on all faiths and traditions, from Zoroaster to existentialism. It covers the different ages of man, the stages of life, and is an ideal reference work and long term companion, a source of inspiration for the journey of life.

Frequently adopting a light touch it also makes a distinction between the Higher Wisdom, which consists of pointers leading to the understanding of philosophical and metaphysical truth, and practical wisdom, which consists of intelligent skills applicable to all fields of ordinary everyday life. So Germaine Greer and Hilary Rodham Clinton have their place alongside Aristotle and Sartre.

The carefully chosen quotations make this book the perfect bedside dipper, and will refresh the spirit of all who are willing to bathe in the ocean of the world's wisdom.

Few individuals have as wide an acquaintance with the world's traditions and scriptures as *Alan Jacobs*. He is Chairperson of the Ramana Maharshi Foundation (UK), editor of *Poetry of the Spirit*, and has translated *The Bhagavad Gita* (O Books), *The Principal Upanishads* (O Books) and *The Wisdom of Marcus Aurelius* (O Books).

1 905047 07 X
£19.95/$29.95

Reiki Mastery

For Second Degree Students and Masters

David Vennells

Reiki has many levels and forms, and has changed along the way from the pure, "original" practice of its Buddhist founder, Dr. Mikao Usui. Advanced Reiki, especially above First Degree, is about "facing the mirror," the inner mirror of our own mind. As we progress with our spiritual practice we can begin to clean away the layers of misconception that colour the way we view ourselves, others and the world around us. This is a compassionate, wise, handbook to making the most of the Life Force Energy that surrounds and informs us all.

David Vennells is a Buddhist teacher of Reiki and the author of *Reiki for Beginners*, *Bach Flower Remedies for Beginners*, *Reflexology for Beginners*.

1-903816-70-X
£9.99/$14.95

The Secret Journey
Poems and prayers from around the world
Susan Skinner

A gift book for the young in heart and spirit

These prayers, verses and invocations are drawn from many faiths and many nations but they all reflect the same mystery: the mystery our passage from birth, through life, to death. We are born from the unknown. Our life, except perhaps to our friends and family, is a secret journey of joy and sorrow. Our death is shrouded in questions.

In the words of St Paul, "now we see through a glass darkly.." But we *do* see some things, if we respond to the spirit within. Most faiths, personal or communal, acknowledge the inspiration of the spiritual life founded on truth, love and compassion.

This anthology is a small reflection of the inspired and enlightening words that have been passed on down the centuries, throughout the world. They sing to the child within us all, to the spirit which always remains open and free and clear-sighted. In the words of Master Eckhart: "The eye with which I see God is the same eye with which God sees me."

Each reflection is stunningly illustrated in full colour, making this an ideal gift book for the young and anyone starting on the spiritual journey, or seeking images and verses for inspiration and meditation. A map and short introduction to the world religions, along with notes on sources, make it a useful addition to all libraries in homes and schools.

Susan Skinner is an artist who has made a life long study of world religions, working their themes into exquisite images. She lives near Hastings, England.

1 905047 08 8
£11.99/$16.95

The Wave

A life-changing journey into the heart and mind of the Cosmos.

Dr Jude Currivan

Pioneering science and the wisdom teachings of many traditions agree – consciousness expresses itself as energy. All energies are manifested as waves – and it is from the vast and ever changing interaction of these waves of energy that the entire Cosmos, at all levels of experience, is continuously created.

In easily accessible terms, *The Wave* explains the profound interconnectedness and harmony of the universe and reveals its underlying principles. Powerfully combining leading edge research with the perennial wisdom of all ages, it reconciles science and spirit into a universal model of consciousness. It describes how we co-create our realities and how the Cosmos affects all life on Earth. It rediscovers the ancient knowledge that birthed feng shui and astrology and perceived the harmony of sacred geometry, music and number. It clarifies the meaning behind a multitude of metaphysical teachings and the common principles underlying the many techniques of energy healing.

The Wave offers not only an explanation of how the universe is as it is, but why the world is as it is and how we can live in harmony with it and ourselves.

Above all, *The Wave* explains the power of love, and in marrying heart and mind, it births a creative and empowering spirituality from their union.

Dr Jude Currivan has a Masters Degree in Physics, specialising in cosmology and quantum physics and a PhD in Archaeology, researching ancient cosmologies, and has studied consciousness and metaphysics from childhood. Moving on from a highly successful international business career in the mid 1990s, she has worked with the shamans and elders of many wisdom traditions, is a healer and teacher at the College of Psychic Studies in London and a master dowser. She travels and teaches worldwide.

1 905047 33 9
£11.99/$19.95

Good As New
A radical re-telling of the Christian Scriptures
John Henson

This radical new translation conveys the early Christian scriptures in the idiom of today. It is "inclusive," following the principles which Jesus adopted in relation to his culture. It is women, gay and sinner friendly. It follows principles of cultural and contextual translation. It also returns to the selection of books that modern scholarship now agrees were held in most esteem by the early Church.

A presentation of extraordinary power. Rowan Williams, Archbishop of Canterbury

I can't rate this version of the Christian scriptures highly enough. It is amazingly fresh, imaginative, engaging and bold. Adrian Thatcher, Professor of Applied Theology, College of St Mark and St John, Plymouth

I found this a literally shocking read. It made me think, it made me laugh, it made me cry, it made me angry and it made me joyful. It made me feel like an early Christian hearing these texts for the first time. Elizabeth Stuart, Professor of Christian Theology, King Alfred's College, Winchester

It spoke to me with a powerful relevancy that challenged me to re-think all the things that I have been taught. Tony Campolo, Professor Emeritus of Sociology, Eastern University

With an extraordinary vigour and immediacy, Good As New *constantly challenges, surprises and delights you. Over and over again you feel like you're reading about Jesus for the first time.* Ship of Fools

John Henson, a retired evangelical Baptist minister, has co-ordinated this translation over the last 12 years on behalf of *ONE for Christian Exploration*, a network of radical Christians and over twenty organisations in the UK

1-903816-74-2
£19.99/$29.95 hb

1-90504711-8
£11.99/$19.95 pb

O

is a symbol of the world,
of oneness and unity. O Books
explores the many paths of wholeness and spiritual understanding which
different traditions have developed down
the ages. It aims to bring this knowledge in
accessible form, to a general readership, pro-
viding practical spirituality to today's seekers.

For the full list of over 200 titles covering:
ACADEMIC/THEOLOGY • ANGELS • ASTROLOGY/
NUMEROLOGY • BIOGRAPHY/AUTOBIOGRAPHY
• BUDDHISM/ENLIGHTENMENT • BUSINESS/LEADERSHIP/
WISDOM • CELTIC/DRUID/PAGAN • CHANNELLING
• CHRISTIANITY; EARLY • CHRISTIANITY; TRADITIONAL
• CHRISTIANITY; PROGRESSIVE • CHRISTIANITY;
DEVOTIONAL • CHILDREN'S SPIRITUALITY • CHILDREN'S
BIBLE STORIES • CHILDREN'S BOARD/NOVELTY • CREATIVE
SPIRITUALITY • CURRENT AFFAIRS/RELIGIOUS • ECONOMY/
POLITICS/SUSTAINABILITY • ENVIRONMENT/EARTH
• FICTION • GODDESS/FEMININE • HEALTH/FITNESS
• HEALING/REIKI • HINDUISM/ADVAITA/VEDANTA
• HISTORY/ARCHAEOLOGY • HOLISTIC SPIRITUALITY
• INTERFAITH/ECUMENICAL • ISLAM/SUFISM
• JUDAISM/CHRISTIANITY • MEDITATION/PRAYER
• MYSTERY/PARANORMAL • MYSTICISM • MYTHS
• POETRY • RELATIONSHIPS/LOVE • RELIGION/
PHILOSOPHY • SCHOOL TITLES • SCIENCE/
RELIGION • SELF-HELP/PSYCHOLOGY
• SPIRITUAL SEARCH • WORLD
RELIGIONS/SCRIPTURES • YOGA

**Please visit our website,
www.O-books.net**